100 facts

GREAT SCIENTISTS

John Farndon

Consultant: Clint Twist

Miles
Kelly

First published in 2012 by Miles Kelly Publishing Ltd
Harding's Barn, Bardfield End Green, Thaxted, Essex, CM6 3PX, UK

Copyright © Miles Kelly Publishing Ltd 2012

This edition printed 2014

10 9 8 7 6 5 4 3

Publishing Director Belinda Gallagher
Creative Director Jo Cowan
Editorial Director Rosie Neave
Volume Designer Andrea Slane
Cover Designer Kayleigh Allen
Image Manager Liberty Newton
Indexer Jane Parker
Production Manager Elizabeth Collins
Reprographics Stephan Davis, Jennifer Cozens, Thom Allaway
Assets Lorraine King

ISBN 978-1-84810-533-1

Printed in China

British Library Cataloguing-in-Publication Data
A catalogue record for this book is available from the British Library

ACKNOWLEDGEMENTS

The publishers would like to thank the following artists who have contributed to this book:

Julian Baker at JB Illustrations, Mike Foster at Maltings Partnership, Mike Saunders

All other artwork from the Miles Kelly Artwork Bank

The publishers would like to thank the following sources for the use of their photographs:

t = top, b = bottom, l = left, r = right, c = centre, bg = background

Cover Front: Topfoto.co.uk; Back: brandonht/shutterstock.com, Antonio Abrignani/shutterstock.com

Alamy 6(l) Guy Bell; 29(c) Photo Researchers; 34(bl) Pictorial Press Ltd

Corbis 8(b) Blue Lantern Studio

Fotolia.com 10 MalDix; 10(bg) Alexey Khromushin

Getty Images 6(t) Will & Deni McIntyre; 12(c) Stocktrek Images; 15(t) Jason Reed; 16(t) Mark Ralston, (c) Barcroft Media/Contributor; 25(b) David Fox; 26 (tr) Gaston Melingue

NASA 34(c) NASA/JPL/California Institute of Technology; 35(c) NASA/JPL-Caltech; 38(t) NASA/JPL-Caltech

Rex Features 37(cr) Jason Rasgon

Science Photo Library 4(c) Anakao Press/Look at Sciences; 10 (c) Christian Jegou Publiphoto Diffusion; 20(br) Sheila Terry; 23(br) Peter Menzel; 25(t) Javier Trueba; 26(c) Jacopin; 30(c) U.S. Navy; 33(t) Mikkel Juul Jensen; 33(bl) Lawrence Livermore; 33(tr) Harvard College Observatory; 38(b) National Institute of Standards and Technlogy; 39(t) Thomas Deerinck, NCMIR; 39(b) David Parker

Shutterstock.com throughout paper labels by kanate; white paper by nuttakit; lined paper by happydancing; 1 iDesign; 3(b) XYZ; 5(b) Cameramannz; 9(bg) pixeldreams.eu; (br) Maridav; 10(tr) c.; 10(tl) Janaka Dharmasena; 11(bl) Suzan Oschmann; 13(b) Olegusk; 13(c) Ana del Castillo; 14(bg) basel101658, (tl) D. Kucharski & K. Kucharska, (c) Jubal Harshaw; 15(b) argus; 16(bg) Chepko Danil Vitalevich, (b) testing; 17(tr), (bl) koya979; 18(cl) Gerasia, (bl) vovan, (bg) beboy; 19 (tr) thoron; 20(tl) JonMilnes, (c) Mazzzur; 21(c) omer cicek, (t) bonchan, Arturo Limon, Denis Selivanov, (br) fzd.it; 22(bg) Molodec, (bl) Gunnar Pippel; 23(tr) Gunnar Pippel; 24(t) Andy Lidstone, (c) AridOcean, (b) Jason Duggan, Brandelet; 25(b) Mazzzur; 27(t) Fotocrisis; 28(bg) Stephen Aaron Rees; 30(bl) MrJafari, Stephen Aaron Rees; 33(br) wanchai; 36(bl) Lisa F. Young; 37(t) Andrey Yurlov, (b) Linda Z Ryan

Topfoto 13(tr) World History Archive; 14(bl) The Granger Collection; 17(c) The Granger Collection; 22(tr) The Granger Collection; 27(b) The British Library/HIP; 29(t) World History Archive

All other photographs are from:

Corel, digitalSTOCK, digitalvision, John Foxx, PhotoAlto, PhotoDisc, PhotoEssentials, PhotoPro, Stockbyte

Every effort has been made to acknowledge the source and copyright holder of each picture. Miles Kelly Publishing apologises for any unintentional errors or omissions.

Made with paper from a sustainable forest

www.mileskelly.net
info@mileskelly.net

CONTENTS

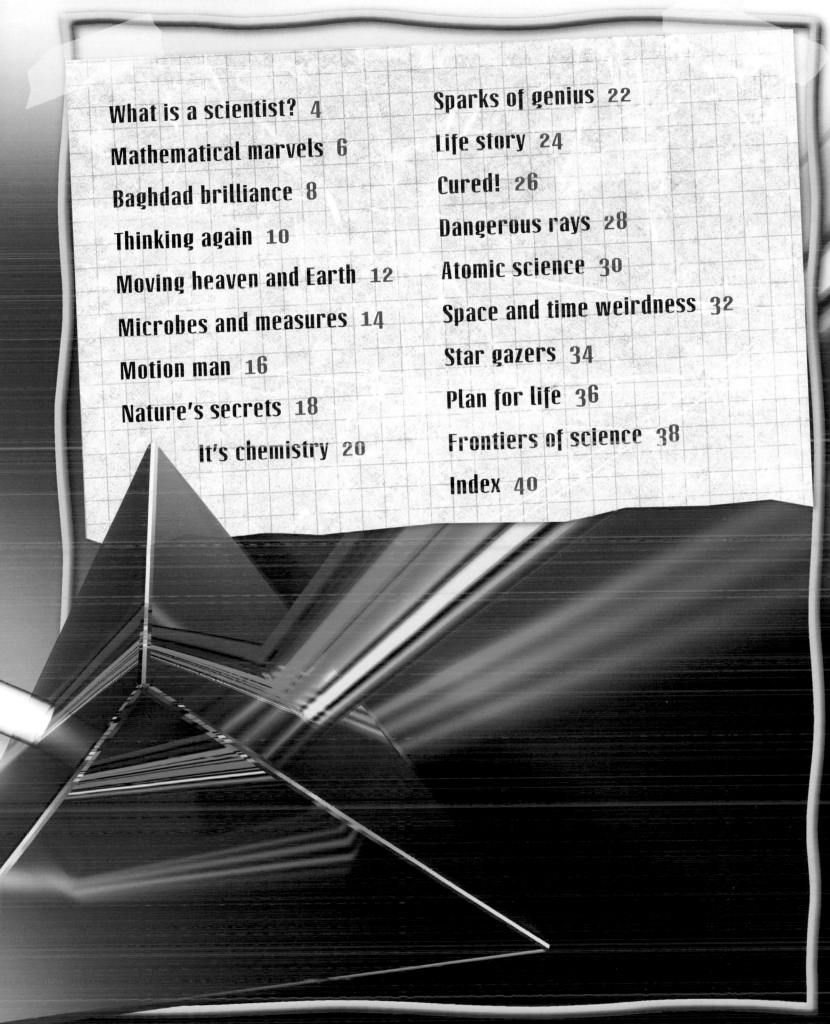

What is a scientist?

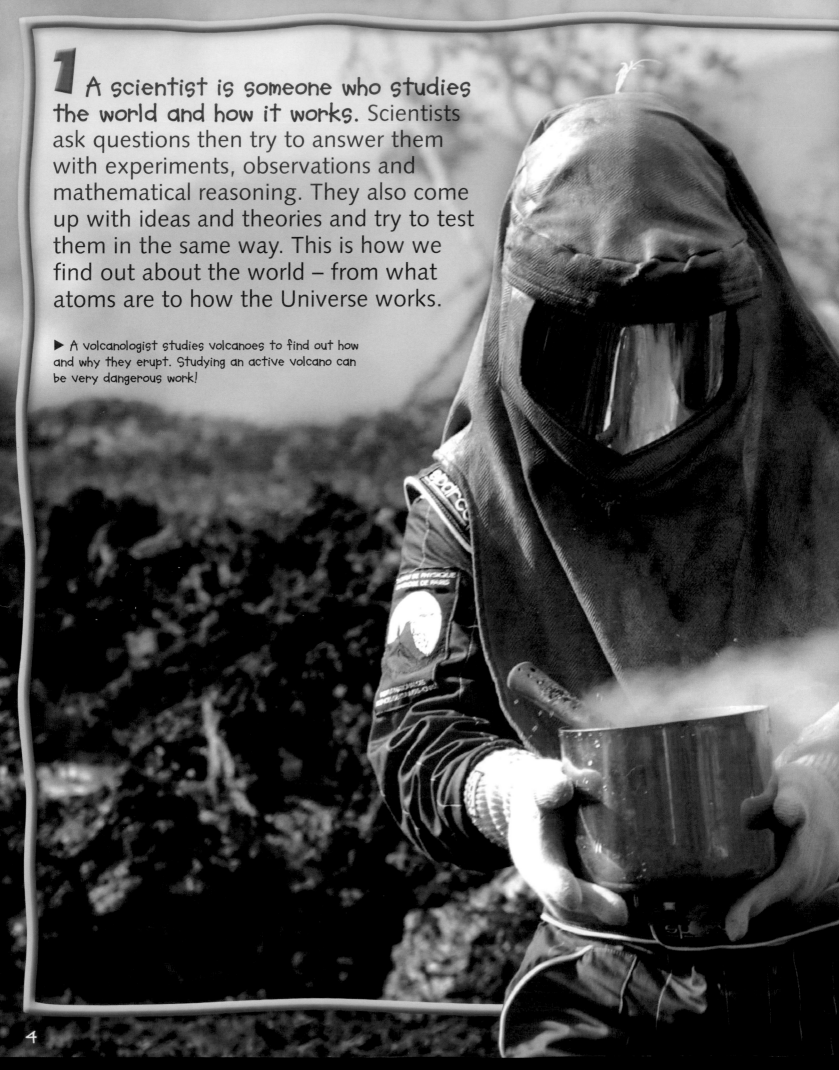

1 A scientist is someone who studies the world and how it works. Scientists ask questions then try to answer them with experiments, observations and mathematical reasoning. They also come up with ideas and theories and try to test them in the same way. This is how we find out about the world – from what atoms are to how the Universe works.

▶ A volcanologist studies volcanoes to find out how and why they erupt. Studying an active volcano can be very dangerous work!

2 Scientific ideas are constantly changing. What scientists think is true in one age may be questioned in the next. Just a century ago, astronomers thought the Universe was no bigger than our Milky Way Galaxy. We now know the Universe is much vaster, with more than 500 billion galaxies.

3 In the past, scientists often studied a wide range of subjects. In fact, the word 'scientist' was not widely used until 1830. Most of the great scientists in this book from before that time were called 'natural philosophers'.

▶ There are many different kinds of scientist. They specialize in different fields, such as particle physicists who study atoms and microbiologists who study microscopic life.

Life sciences

Botany.................. Botanists study plants in nature and the laboratory

Zoology............... Zoologists study animals in nature and the laboratory

Genetics............... Genetics is the science of how living things pass on features to offspring

Medicine............... Medicine is the science of understanding and healing the human body

Physical Sciences

Physics.................. Physicists study matter and forces and how they move through space and time

Chemistry............. Chemists study substances and how they react with each other

Astronomy........... Astronomers study space – from moons and planets to stars and galaxies

Earth Sciences

Geology.............. Geologists study rocks and minerals and how the Earth works

Oceanography........ Oceanographers study the oceans and ocean currents and tides

Palaeontology...... Palaeontologists study prehistoric life and fossils

Meteorology......... Meteorologists study the weather, climate and changes in the atmosphere

Mathematical marvels

4 About 10,000 years ago, people in the Middle East began to farm. They built great civilizations, such as ancient Egypt, and developed numbers, which helped to keep a record of things. They discovered that numbers could be used to work things out, such as fair shares or the area of a field. This is how mathematics began.

▼ The ancient Egyptians built the pyramids with amazing accuracy. They could work out the height of a pyramid just from the length of its shadow.

Euclid
Greek c. 300 BC

◀ The Shard in London is a brand new building, which will be complete in 2012. Modern engineers have based their ideas on Euclid's ancient proof.

5 In ancient Greece, mathematicians worked out things such as the areas of triangles. They set out logical proof of their ideas. The greatest mathematician was Euclid, whose book 'Elements' still provides basic skills used by engineers and builders today.

Archimedes
Greek 287–212 BC

6 Archimedes thought about problems in a scientific way. He came up with theories that could be proved or disproved by experiments and mathematics. Archimedes proved that the power of a lever (a simple machine) to move a load depends on how far from its pivot point (point of rotation) you apply your effort.

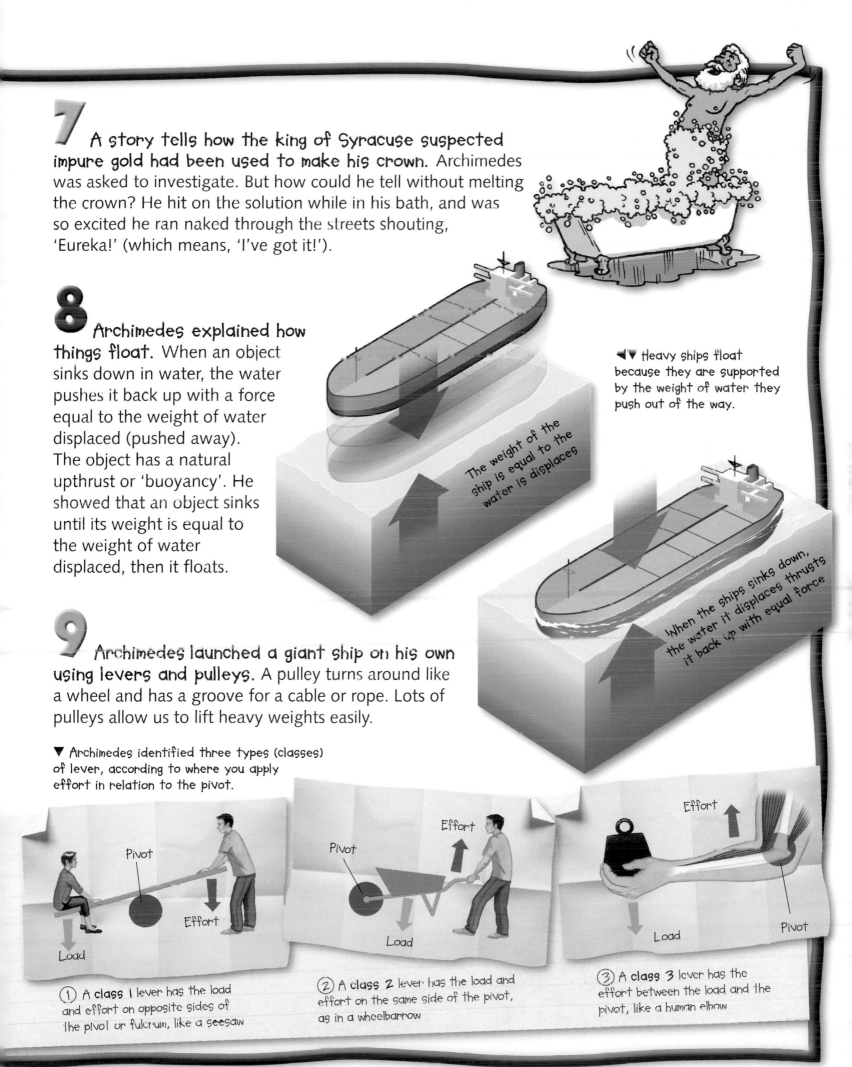

7 A story tells how the king of Syracuse suspected impure gold had been used to make his crown. Archimedes was asked to investigate. But how could he tell without melting the crown? He hit on the solution while in his bath, and was so excited he ran naked through the streets shouting, 'Eureka!' (which means, 'I've got it!').

8 Archimedes explained how things float. When an object sinks down in water, the water pushes it back up with a force equal to the weight of water displaced (pushed away). The object has a natural upthrust or 'buoyancy'. He showed that an object sinks until its weight is equal to the weight of water displaced, then it floats.

◄▼ Heavy ships float because they are supported by the weight of water they push out of the way.

The weight of the ship is equal to the water is displaces

When the ships sinks down, the water it displaces thrusts it back up with equal force

9 Archimedes launched a giant ship on his own using levers and pulleys. A pulley turns around like a wheel and has a groove for a cable or rope. Lots of pulleys allow us to lift heavy weights easily.

▼ Archimedes identified three types (classes) of lever, according to where you apply effort in relation to the pivot.

Pivot
Effort
Load

① A class 1 lever has the load and effort on opposite sides of the pivot or fulcrum, like a seesaw

Pivot
Effort
Load

② A class 2 lever has the load and effort on the same side of the pivot, as in a wheelbarrow

Effort
Load
Pivot

③ A class 3 lever has the effort between the load and the pivot, like a human elbow

Baghdad brilliance

10 When Muhammad began to teach the religion of Islam in the 600s, he charged followers to search for knowledge. Baghdad and other Islamic cities became centres of learning. Ibn Sina studied everything from philosophy to physics. He not only identified the main forms of energy and the idea of force, he wrote a book, *The Canon of Medicine*, which became the doctors' bible for 600 years.

Ibn Sina Avicenna
Persian c. 980–1037

QUIZ

1. What did the astrolabe measure?
2. What is distillation used for today?
3. What does algebra use to replace unknown numbers in calculations?

Answers:
1. Angles 2. For refining oil and alcohol 3. Symbols or letters

Muhammad al-Fazari
Arabic or Persian
Died 796 or 806

11 Muslims needed to know the true direction of Muhammad's birthplace. So scientists developed astronomical instruments to map the stars. The astrolabe was invented by astronomer Muhammad al-Fazari. It measured angles by sight, and skilled users could work out directions from the position of stars alone.

▶ Muslim astronomers mapped the stars and their movements very accurately.

12 Jabir ibn Hayyan (Geber) stirred and heated chemicals together in measured quantities to see how they interacted. Jabir also found he could purify liquids by boiling them and collecting the droplets of steam. This is called distillation and is used today for refining oil and alcoholic spirits.

Jabir ibn Hayyan (Geber)
Persian 721–815

13 Roman numerals were awkward to use for large numbers. So in the 8th century, after studying Indian Hindu numbers, al-Khwarizmi introduced the Arabic numerals we now use around the world. Roman numerals need seven figures to give a number as small as 38 (XXXVIII). With seven figures, Arabic numerals can give nearly ten million!

al-Khwarizmi
Arabic or Persian
c.780–850

▲ As well distillation, Geber discovered acids that were strong enough to dissolve metals.

▶ Roman numerals were built up by adding lines. Arabic numerals use symbols for one to 10, which is simpler.

14 Al-Khwarizmi created the maths known as algebra. Algebra uses symbols or letters to replace unknown numbers in calculations. Mathematicians can work out the unknown numbers by putting the symbols in standard 'recipes' called equations. Algebra is part of nearly all scientific calculations.

15 When al-Khwarizmi's name was written in Latin it was spelt 'Algoritmi'. This name has given us the word 'algorithms'. Algorithms are logical step-by-step mathematical sequences, and it was al-Khwarizmi who first developed the idea. Algorithms are now the basis of all computer programs.

Ancient Roman	Modern Hindu-Arabic
I	1
II	2
III	3
IV	4
V	5
VI	6
VII	7
VIII	8
IX	9
X	10

Thinking again

16 In the 1400s, Islamic science reached Europe. The ideas of ancient Greece and Rome were rediscovered, and people like Leonardo da Vinci were excited. They realized that by studying the world, they might learn how it works.

17 You might think helicopters and cars are modern ideas – but Leonardo drew designs for them 500 years ago. His sketches for a hang-glider type flying machine are so detailed that experts recently built one for real – and found that it just about worked.

▼ A scientific genius, Leonardo made brilliant notes and drawings on everything from geology to flying machines.

▼ Leonardo was way ahead of his time, making models to study how rivers flowed.

18 Leonardo wrote to the Duke of Milan offering his services as an engineer. He had an idea for an armoured car or tank. Tanks were only first used in World War I (1914–1918). Yet there is a picture of one in Leonardo's notebooks from the 1480s.

19 To draw human figures accurately, artists studied the human body. To show the body's inner layers, Leonardo developed a way of drawing cross-sections and 3D versions of muscles.

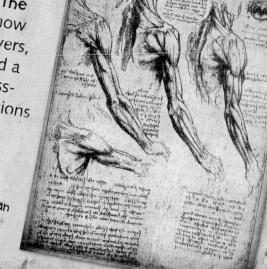

► Leonardo drew highly accurate diagrams of the human muscular system.

20 Early physicians learned about the body (often wrongly) from ancient books – especially those of Galen (129–199), a Roman doctor. Andreas Vesalius realized the only way to find out was to cut up real corpses (dead bodies). As he did this, he got artist Jan van Calcar to draw what he found. They made the first accurate book of human anatomy (the way the body is put together) in 1543.

► As Vesalius carefully cut up bodies, Jan van Calcar made drawings to build up an accurate guide to human anatomy.

Andreas Vesalius
Dutch 1514–1564

21 Many scientists studied in Padua in Italy in the 1500s, including English physician William Harvey. When Harvey returned to England, he studied how blood flowed through the body. He found that it doesn't flow to and fro like tides as Galen said. Instead it is pumped by the heart non-stop around the body through tubes called arteries and veins.

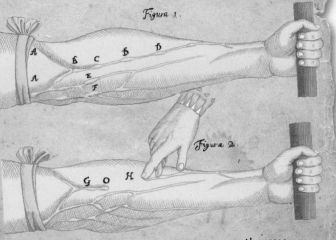

▲ Careful experiments showed William Harvey that blood flowed around the body again and again.

William Harvey
English 1578–1657

Moving heaven and Earth

22 Until the 1400s, most people thought the Earth was fixed in the middle of the Universe. They believed the Sun, Moon, planets and stars revolved around it. Astronomers came up with elaborate circle patterns to explain this. Then in 1514, Nicolas Copernicus realized the truth – the Earth goes around the Sun, along with the Moon and other planets.

I DON'T BELIEVE IT!

Catholic church leaders were so upset when Galileo said the Earth goes around the Sun they arrested him. He was not officially forgiven until 1992.

Nicolas Copernicus
Polish 1473–1543

Johannes Kepler
German 1571–1630

▲ Copernicus was the first to suggest that the Earth isn't still but moves around the Sun, along with all the other planets.

KEY

1	Mercury		5	Jupiter
2	Venus		6	Saturn
3	Earth		7	Uranus
4	Mars		8	Neptune

23 Copernicus' idea that the Earth goes around the Sun didn't seem to fit with observations. So even the cleverest astronomers thought he might be wrong. Their mistake was to assume that the planets' orbits (paths) are circular. German astronomer Johannes Kepler realized that their orbits are not circles, but an ellipse (oval). With elliptical orbits, the observations match Copernicus' idea exactly.

24 People wanted proof that Copernicus was right. The man to give it was Italian genius, Galileo Galilei. He invented the telescope so he could see the night sky better than anyone had before. Today, telescopes are revealing more and more to us about the Universe.

▼ Many church leaders did not believe that what Galileo showed them through the telescope was actually real.

Galileo Galilei
Italian 1564–1642

25 The telescope showed that Copernicus was right. Galileo saw moons circling Jupiter, proving that the Earth is not the centre of everything. Light and shadows that Galileo saw on Venus showed that it moves around the Sun, not the Earth.

◄ Galileo reportedly dropped a 10-pound weight and a one-pound weight off the Leaning Tower of Pisa, and proved that both fall at the same speed.

26 Galileo's greatest achievement was to show that things get faster as they fall. It sounds obvious, but it took Galileo's genius to realize that they gain speed evenly – and he proved this by timing how fast balls run down a wooden slope. This was crucial to our understanding of how things move, from cars to planets.

Microbes and measures

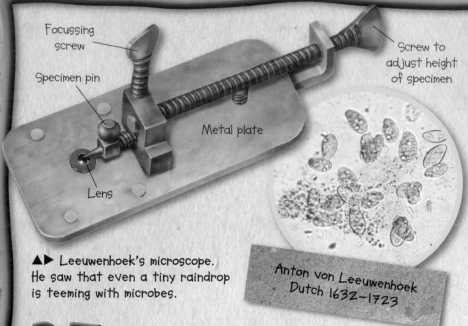

Focussing screw

Screw to adjust height of specimen

Specimen pin

Metal plate

Lens

▲▶ Leeuwenhoek's microscope. He saw that even a tiny raindrop is teeming with microbes.

Anton von Leeuwenhoek Dutch 1632–1723

28 Robert Hooke was another microscope pioneer and saw that living things are made from tiny 'parcels'. He called them cells, because to him they looked like tiny rows of rooms or cells that monks lived in. Hooke also invented the hearing aid and the anemometer (for measuring wind speed).

27 No one knew there was life too small to see – until Anton von Leeuwenhoek looked through his microscope in the 1670s. Leeuwenhoek made his own microscope, with lenses that could magnify up to 270 times.

▶▼ Through his microscope, Hooke saw that living things are made up from tiny packages, which he named 'cells'.

Robert Hooke English 1635–1703

Christiaan Huygens Dutch 1629–1695

29 Before the 1600s, people could only tell the time to within ten minutes. But in 1658 Christiaan Huygens perfected a clock that kept time with a swinging weight, or pendulum. It was the world's first accurate clock, so precise it could keep time to within a minute over a week.

◀ Huygens also worked out the maths of pendulums that helps us understand how planets move.

30 Like Galileo, Huygens made his own telescope. Peering through it, he saw that the planet Saturn had a moon, too, later called Titan. He also realized that what had looked to Galileo like ears on Saturn were part of a flat hoop or ring running around it.

▼ We now know that Saturn's rings are made up of tiny particles of water, ice and dust.

René Descartes
French 1596–1650

31 French philosopher René Descartes came up with the idea of graphs. Graphs are a way of looking at things that are changing together. When something accelerates, both speed and time change. On a graph, you draw the changes as a simple line called a curve.

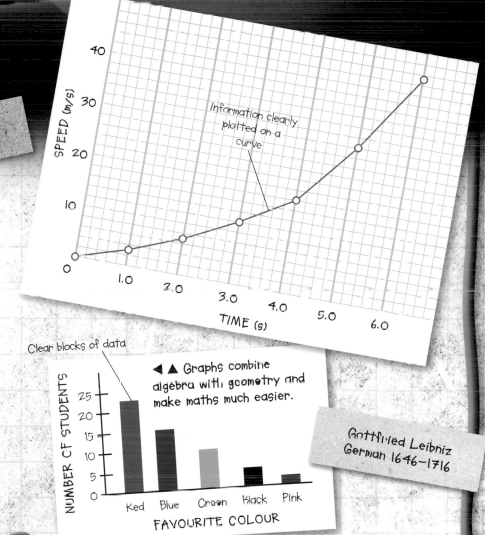

Information clearly plotted on a curve

Clear blocks of data

◄▲ Graphs combine algebra with geometry and make maths much easier.

Gottfried Leibniz
German 1646–1716

32 Most things in nature move at varying speeds. To study them, Isaac Newton and Gottfried Leibnitz devised a kind of maths called calculus. Calculus helps you find out how fast something is moving at any one instant – a time so short that it seems to move no distance at all

Motion man

Sir Isaac Newton
English 1643–1727

33 Isaac Newton discovered that every movement in the Universe obeys three rules, known as the Laws of Motion. They sum up what it takes to get something moving or to stop (1st Law), to make something move faster or slower, or change direction (2nd Law), and how the movement of one thing affects another (3rd Law).

LAW 1: An object won't move unless something forces it to. It will go on moving at the same speed and in the same direction unless forced to change. This is called inertia.

LAW 2: The greater the mass of an object, the more force is needed to make it speed up, slow down or change direction.

▶▲ Scientists can use these laws to work out everything – from the way a diver pushes off from a springboard to the rotation of a galaxy.

34 Newton also discovered gravity – the force of attraction between all matter. He knew that nothing strays from its course without being forced to. So when something starts to fall, it must be forced to. That force is gravity, the same force that holds planets in orbit around the Sun.

MARBLE MOTION

Demonstrate Newton's Third Law of Motion with marbles or the balls on a pool table. Roll one ball or marble into another – and watch how when they collide, one ball moves one way and the other ball moves the other way.

35 Early telescopes worked by using lenses to refract (bend) rays of light together. Newton used curved mirrors instead of lenses to throw light rays back on themselves, creating a compact, powerful telescope. Most telescopes today are Newtonian or 'reflecting' telescopes.

LAW 3: For every action, there is an equal opposite reaction – in other words, when something pushes off in one direction, the thing it's pushing from is pushed back with equal force in the opposite direction.

36 Sunlight is colourless or white – so where do all the colours come from? Newton realized that sunlight contains all the colours, mixed up. He proved it using a prism, a triangular block of glass.

▼ When sunlight shines through a prism, its rays are bent, each colour to a different degree. When the light emerges from the far side of the prism, it splits into a spectrum – all the colours of the rainbow.

37 Newton was the first modern scientist, but he wrote works of alchemy – a cross between science, magic and astrology. Alchemists wanted to find the 'philosopher's stone' (a substance that could turn metal to gold) and the 'elixir of life' (a liquid that keeps you young forever). They wrote in code to keep their work secret, and Newton's notebooks are impossible to understand.

Nature's secrets

38 Today, all living things are organized into clear groups – thanks to biologist Carolus Linnaeus. Before this, animals and plants were listed at best alphabetically. Since creatures have different names in different places, this led to chaos.

39 Linnaeus gave all species a two-part scientific name in Latin. The first part is the group it belongs to, and the second is an individual name (like your name and family name, only with the family name first). For example, the swamp rabbit is *Sylvilagus aquaticus*.

PARTS OF A FLOWERING PLANT

Anther (male part)

Stigma (female part)

▲ Linnaeus realized that flowering plants can be classified by the shape of their male and female parts.

Carolus Linnaeus
Swedish 1707–1778

James Hutton
Scottish 1726–1797

▲ A volcanic eruption is a short, sharp force of nature. James Hutton concluded that the landscape is shaped mostly by more gradual forces such as running rivers.

40 People once thought the Earth was just a few thousand years old and the entire landscape was shaped by a few short, huge disasters. But in his book *Theory of the Earth*, published in 1788, James Hutton showed how the Earth has been shaped gradually over millions of years by milder forces, such as running rivers.

HOMEMADE FOSSIL

Make your own fossil by pressing a snail shell or an old bone into tightly compressed fine sand. Take out the shell or bone, then pour runny plaster or wall filler into the mould left behind. Leave the plaster to set, then dig up your fossil!

41 Charles Lyell showed how rocks tell the story of Earth's past. Rock layers form one on top of the other over time and can be read by a geologist like pages in a book. They contain fossils – the remains of once living things turned to stone – showing what creatures were alive when each layer formed.

▲ The first dinosaur fossils were discovered in rock in Lyell's lifetime.

Mary Anning
English 1799–1847

42 Mary Anning hunted for fossils on the shore at Lyme Regis in England, one of the world's richest fossil sites. At the age of 12, she found the skeleton of an ichthyosaur, a dolphin-shaped creature from the time of the dinosaurs – though no one knew about dinosaurs at the time. She went on to find the first fossils of a giant swimming reptile, *Plesiosaurus*, and the first flying reptiles, or pterosaurs.

▲ Mary Anning discovered fossils of a giant swimming reptile, a plesiosaur, which may have looked like this.

William Buckland
English 1784–1856

43 In 1824, William Buckland wrote the first scientific description of a dinosaur fossil, *Megalosaurus*. This meat-eater was 9 metres long and weighed as much as an elephant. People were astonished such creatures had ever lived, but soon more fossils were found.

▶ Buckland named *Megalosaurus* in 1824. It was not until 1842 that the term 'dinosaur' was first used.

It's chemistry

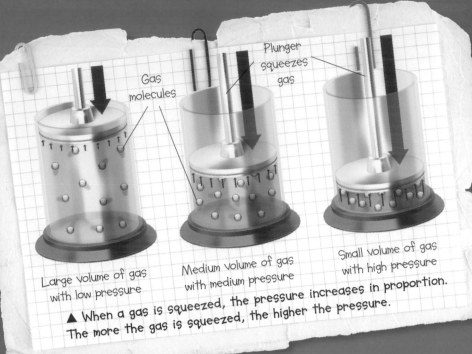

Gas molecules

Plunger squeezes gas

Large volume of gas with low pressure

Medium volume of gas with medium pressure

Small volume of gas with high pressure

▲ When a gas is squeezed, the pressure increases in proportion. The more the gas is squeezed, the higher the pressure.

Robert Boyle
Irish 1627–1691

▲ Boyle's Law shows that the pressure of gases in a diver's suit and body rises as he descends, due to the weight of the water.

44 **Robert Boyle was the first great chemist of modern times.** With Boyle's Law, he showed that when a gas is compressed its pressure increases at the same rate. He also suggested that everything is made up from basic chemicals or 'elements', which can join together in different ways.

▼ Lavoisier showed that, like solid elements, two gases can join to make a new substance, or compound. Here he is experimenting with hydrogen and oxygen, to produce water.

45 People once believed air was not a substance. But Antoine Lavoisier realized substances can exist in three different states – solid, liquid and gas – and if gases are substances, then so is air. He found air is a mix of gases, mostly nitrogen and oxygen.

46 Scientists used to think that everything that burns contained a substance called phlogiston. They thought that as something burned it lost phlogiston. Lavoisier found by careful weighing that tin gains weight when it burns, because it takes in oxygen. So phlogiston couldn't exist. Lavoisier had proved the importance of accurate measurement.

Antoine Lavoisier
French 1743–1794

Cobalt
Co

Copper
Cu

Molybdenum
Mo

Tungsten
W

Aluminium
Al

Antinomy
Sb

47 In 1787, Lavoisier introduced symbols for the different chemical elements. So oxygen is 'O' and hydrogen is 'H'. Lavoisier knew of less than 40 elements. Today, chemists use chemical formulae to identify compounds and the mix of elements of which they are composed. For example, water has the chemical symbol H_2O. This means it has two hydrogen (H) atoms to one oxygen (O).

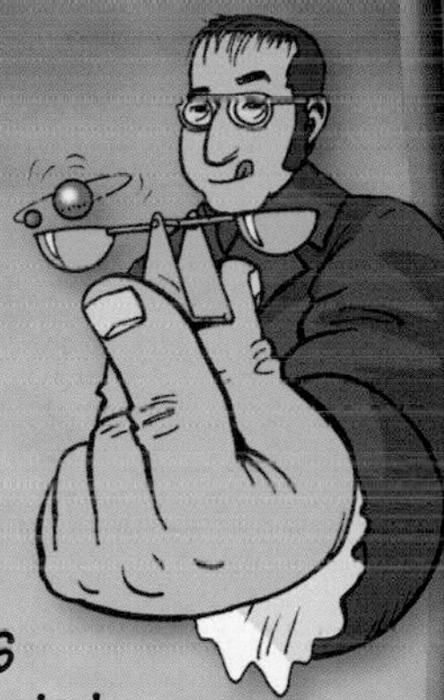

▲▶ Minerals help to make up rocks. Each of these minerals contains a particular metal. The chemical symbols shown here are for each metal.

Mercury
Hg

John Dalton
English 1766–1844

48 Chemist John Dalton realized elements are made from solid particles called atoms. Each element is made from atoms of a certain weight. He found hydrogen to be the lightest, so he assigned it an 'atomic weight' of 1. Dalton's atomic theory of the elements is central to chemistry.

49 In 1869, Dmitri Mendeleyev arranged the elements in a table in order of their atomic weight. He placed them from left to right in rows or 'periods' of seven that revealed a pattern. Elements in the same column (from top to bottom) have similar properties. All elements at one end of each row are reactive metals, while those at the other are unreactive gases.

▶ Elements are arranged in rows called periods in the Periodic Table. Mecury is number 80, in row 6.

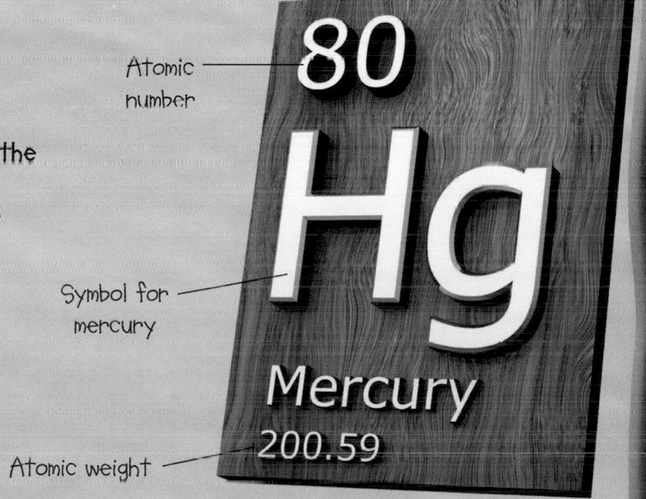

Atomic number

80

Hg

Symbol for mercury

Mercury
200.59

Atomic weight

Dmitri Mendeleyev
Russian 1834–1907

21

Sparks of genius

50 In the 1700s, scientists discovered that rubbing things together can give an electrical charge and may create a spark. Benjamin Franklin wondered if lightning was electrical too. He attached a key to a kite, which he flew during a thunderstorm, and got a similar spark from the key.

▼ A spark flew from the key on Franklin's kite, showing that lightning was electrical.

Benjamin Franklin
American 1706–1790

Luigi Galvani
Italian 1737–1798

51 Luigi Galvani made a dead frog's legs twitch with electricity. He believed, incorrectly, that electricity was made by animals' bodies. Alessandro Volta believed this was just a chemical reaction. In 1800, he used the reaction between 'sandwiches' of disks made of the metals copper and zinc in saltwater to create a battery.

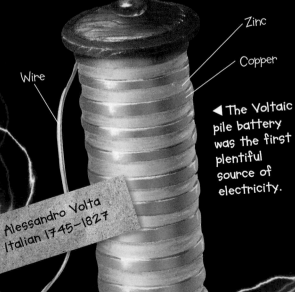

Zinc

Copper

Wire

◄ The Voltaic pile battery was the first plentiful source of electricity.

Alessandro Volta
Italian 1745–1827

Hans Christiaan Øersted
Danish 1777–1851

52 No one realized electricity and magnetism were linked – until physicist Hans Øersted noticed something strange. During a lecture in 1820, he observed that when an electric current was switched on and off, a nearby compass needle swivelled. He went on to confirm with experiments that an electric current creates a magnetic field around it. This effect is known as electromagnetism.

Michael Faraday
English 1791–1867

53 Michael Faraday was fascinated by Øersted's discovery. The following year he showed how the interreaction between a magnet and an electrical current can make a wire move. Faraday and others then went on to use this discovery to create the first electric motors.

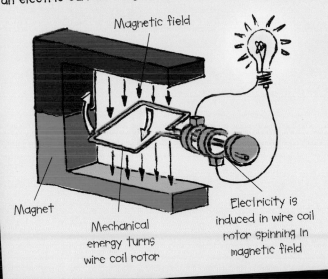

▼ Faraday found that when a wire moves near a magnet, an electric current is generated in it.

Magnetic field

Magnet

Mechanical energy turns wire coil rotor

Electricity is induced in wire coil rotor spinning in magnetic field

QUIZ
1. What makes lightning?
2. Who are volts named after?
3. What is a magnetic field?
4. Who invented electric generators besides Joseph Henry?

Answers:
1. Electricity 2. Alessandro Volta 3. The magnetic area around a magnet 4. Michael Faraday

54 In 1830, Faraday in London and Joseph Henry in New York found that magnets create electricity. When a magnet is moved near an electric circuit, it creates a surge of electricity. Using this idea, machines could be built to generate lots of electricity.

Joseph Henry
American 1797–1878

55 Faraday's experiments with electricity convinced him that all types of electricity were basically the same. It didn't matter if they were produced naturally in Earth's atmosphere in the form of lightning, artificially by chemical reactions in a battery, or by a rotating copper coil inside a magnetic field.

▶ Faraday showed how a cage of metal wire (known as a Faraday cage) could block electrical discharges and protect a person from lightning.

Life story

56 In 1830, Charles Darwin set out on a voyage around the world in the ship *HMS Beagle*. The journey lasted five years, and took in places such as the Galapagos Islands in the Pacific. Darwin recorded the huge range of wildlife he saw, which sowed the seeds of his theory of evolution.

57 Darwin's idea was that evolution (when species gradually change through time) occurs through 'natural selection'. Organisms are all born slightly different. Those born with differences that help them cope better with the conditions are more likely to survive and have offspring. Their special difference is 'naturally selected' and passed on, while others die out.

▼ Cut off from the mainland and from each other, the Galapagos Islands developed a unique range of creatures, helping Darwin develop his ideas.

26p   C. Darwin

▲ Perhaps Darwin's most famous example of natural selection is the Galapagos finch. Each species has evolved a unique beak shape to suit their diets.

SAN SALVADOR

FERNANDINA

SANTA CRUZ

SANTA FE

SAN CRISTOBAL

ISABELA

SANTA MARIA

ESPANOLA

Cormorants on these remote isles lost the ability to fly

Each island has evolved its own kind of giant tortoise

Native fur seals never stray far from the Galapagos shores

24

58 Darwin worked on his idea for 20 years. Naturalists sent him observations, and he received letters from animal breeders. Breeders said they could bring out certain characteristics by selecting the right animals to breed from. That's why there are so many different breeds of dogs.

▲ Darwin concluded that humans and apes, such as chimpanzees, gorillas and orang-utans, all share a common ancestor.

59 In 1858, Alfred Russel Wallace sent Darwin a letter suggesting, like Darwin, that evolution occurs by natural selection. They decided to publish their ideas together, so some say it was Wallace's idea too. But Darwin had already spent 20 years working out the details. In 1859 Darwin told the world about his theory in his book *On the Origin of Species*.

60 Some religious people were upset by Darwin's ideas. They believed all species were created at once by God. They didn't like the idea that humans evolved from apes. The fuss eventually died down, and Darwin's theory is now widely accepted.

▼ Due to natural selection, light-coloured peppered moths are dying out. Darker specimens, which are better hidden on trees darkened by pollution, are more common.

Alfred Russel Wallace
British 1823–1913

Vanishing lighter-coloured moth

Thriving durker-coloured moth

Cured!

61 **People who survived the disease smallpox became immune to a second attack.** This meant their bodies could resist the infection. Doctor Edward Jenner injected his gardener's son with cowpox, a milder disease, to see if it gave the same immunity. It did.

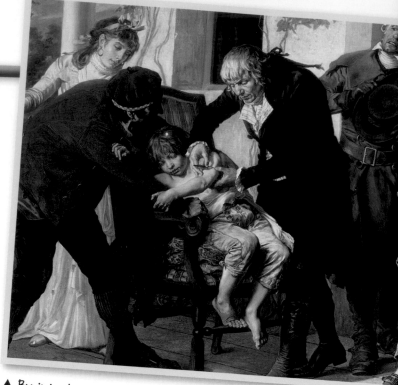

▲ By injecting his gardener's son with cowpox, Edward Jenner had taken the first step towards wiping out the killer disease smallpox.

62 **Before 1850, no one knew dirt in hospitals could spread killer germs.** Countless patients died of infections. Doctor Ignaz Semmelweiss asked students to wash their hands before dealing with patients. This act of simple hygiene helped reduce the number of deaths.

Ignaz Semmelweis
Hungarian 1818–1865

63 **Surgeon Joseph Lister introduced soap to his operations to keep things spotlessly clean.** Cleanliness cut infections during surgery dramatically, and antiseptic techniques are now a vital part of every operation.

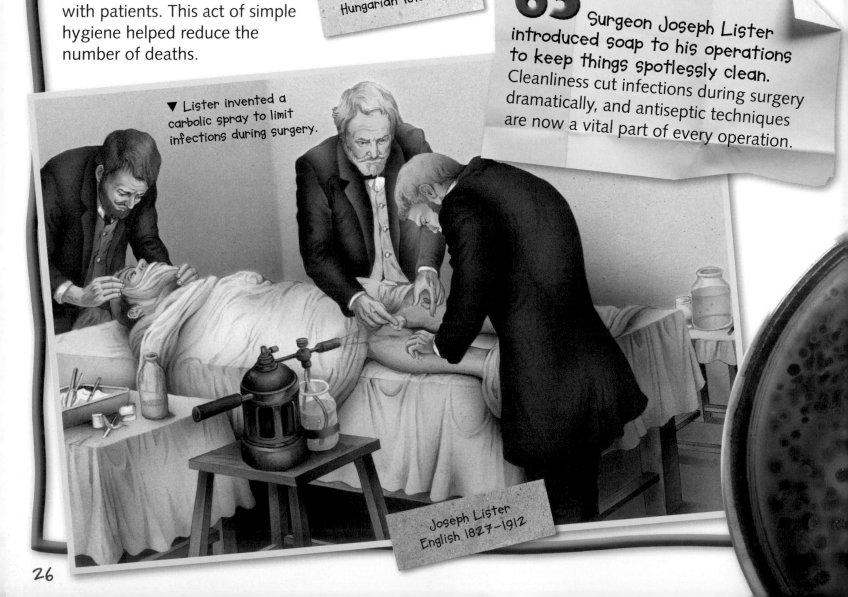

▼ Lister invented a carbolic spray to limit infections during surgery.

Joseph Lister
English 1827–1912

64 The idea that germs cause disease has been around for over 400 years. But it was Louis Pasteur who, with Robert Koch, proved the link in the 1870s. They showed how bacteria spread the sheep disease anthrax.

Louis Pasteur
French 1822–1895

▼ We now know many diseases are spread by microbes — mainly bacteria and viruses. In future they may be targeted by tiny 'nano-robots' placed inside our bodies.

Robert Koch
German 1843–1910

Paul Ehrlich
German 1854–1915

65 Paul Ehrlich believed diseases might be cured by targeting germs with chemical 'magic bullets.' He and student Sahachiro Hato searched for a chemical to kill the bacteria that caused the disease syphilis. They found one called arsphenamine, which wiped out the syphilis germ but left the patient almost unharmed.

Sahachiro Hato
Japanese 1873–1938

Alexander Fleming
Scottish 1881–1955

66 In 1928, Alexander Fleming saw a clue that led to the miracle drugs antibotics. He was culturing (growing) bacteria in dishes in his lab, when he saw that mould growing on one neglected dish had killed the bacteria. Fleming realized that the mould, called *Penicillium notatum*, could be harnessed to fight disease.

◄ Ten years after Fleming discovered the bacteria-killing mould, Howard Florey (1898–1968) and Ernst Chain (1906–1977) created the first antibiotic drug, penicillin.

Dangerous rays

67 In 1886, Heinrich Hertz proved that an electromagnetic current spreads as waves. He made a flickering electric spark jump a gap in an electrical circuit. As the spark flickered, it radiated waves, which set another spark flickering in sync in an aerial receiver. Hertz had discovered radio waves.

Heinrich Hertz
German 1857–1894

② High voltage current jumps a gap in an electric circuit and creates a spark

③ Spark sends out electromagnetic waves

④ Waves induce a tiny spark in aerial receiver

① Coil produces high voltage current

▲ Hertz's experiments with electricity and electromagnetic waves led to the development of the radio.

▼ We now know that the cathode rays in Crookes' glass tube were actually made up of tiny electrical particles.

Cathode rays

Cathode terminal

Anode terminal

Mask

Shadow

68 In the 1870s, William Crookes made a glass tube with nearly all the air sucked out of it. When connected to an electric current, the glass tube glowed. This was because electric charge flowed between the terminals, sending out electromagnetic radiation, which Crookes called cathode rays. A metal mask inside the tube cast a shadow, showing that the rays travelled in straight lines.

William Crookes
English 1832–1919

69 In 1895, Wilhelm Röntgen found that even when he covered a Crookes tube, its rays still made a nearby screen glow. Some rays must be shining through the cover. He tried putting other objects in front of the rays (which he called X-rays) and eventually placed his wife's hand. The rays passed through flesh, but were blocked by bone. Röntgen replaced the screen with photo paper and took the first X-ray photo of his wife's hand.

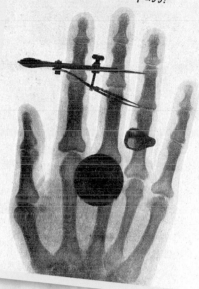

▼ As well as bone, Röntgen discovered that X-rays were blocked by the metal of his wife's jewellery, and a compass!

70 Henri Becquerel found that uranium crystals left on photo paper in a drawer made a photo of themselves. They were releasing or 'radiating' their own energy. He had discovered radioactivity – radiation so energetic it breaks up atoms. This kind of radiation is quite different from electromagnetic radiation and is used to make nuclear bombs.

◄ Marie Curie was the first woman to be awarded a Nobel Prize, in 1903 for physics. She was awarded it again, this time in chemistry, in 1911.

71 Pierre and Marie Curie were fascinated by radioactivity. They discovered two new radioactive elements, radium and polonium. In 1903, they were awarded the Nobel Prize for their work. Marie Curie died from cancer caused by exposure to radioactivity.

Atomic science

Sir Joseph John (JJ) Thomson
English 1856–1940

72 Scientists once thought atoms were the smallest particles. In 1897, JJ Thomson noticed how magnets bent rays from a cathode ray tube. He realized the rays were streams of particles, much smaller than an atom. Thomson wrongly believed these particles or 'electrons' split off from atoms like currents off a bun.

Sir Ernest Rutherford
New Zealand–born British
1871–1937

73 Ernest Rutherford found that radioactivity is the result of atoms breaking up into different atoms, sending out streams of 'alpha' and 'beta' particles. In 1911, he fired streams of alpha particles at gold foil. Most went straight through, but a few bounced back, pushed by the nuclei inside the gold foil atoms. He realized that atoms aren't solid, but largely empty space with a tiny, dense nucleus (core).

▶ Fortunately, all nuclear explosions since the attack on Japan in 1945 have been tests.

Neils Bohr
Danish 1885–1962

74 In 1912, Niels Bohr suggested that different kinds of atom had a certain number of electrons. He thought they buzzed around an atom's nucleus at varying distances, like planets around the Sun. Atoms give out light and lose energy when electrons fall closer to the nucleus. When atoms absorb light, the electrons jump further out.

▶ We now know that electrons are like fuzzy clouds of energy rather than planets.

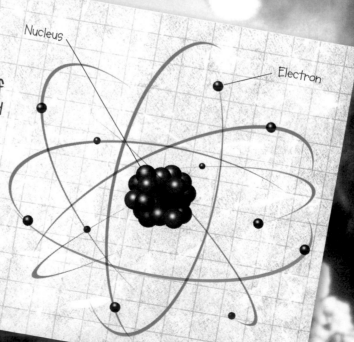

Nucleus

Electron

30

75 In 1918 Rutherford split atoms for the first time. He fired alpha particles at nitrogen gas and found that hydrogen nuclei chipped off the nitrogen nuclei. He realized that all atomic nuclei are clusters of hydrogen nuclei, which he called protons. Fourteen years later, James Chadwick discovered nuclei also have another kind of particle in the nucleus – the neutron.

James Chadwick
English 1891–1974

76 Enrico Fermi fired neutrons at a uranium atom, to see if they'd stick to form a bigger atom. Instead, the uranium atom split into two smaller atoms and released more neutrons, and heat and light energy. Fermi realized that if these neutrons spun off to split more uranium atoms a 'chain reaction' of splitting could occur.

Enrico Fermi
Italian–American
1901–1954

① Neutron fired at nucleus of Uranium atom

◀ Enrico Fermi showed how a chain reaction of an atom splitting could begin with the impact of just a single neutron.

② Nucleus splits in two

④ More neutrons released

Uranium atom

③ Energy released

⑤ Chain reaction occurs

77 During World War II (1939–1945) Fermi created a chain reaction of nuclear splitting, or 'fission'. This unleashed energy to create an incredibly powerful bomb. At Los Alamo, New Mexico, Robert Oppenheimer used this idea to make the first nuclear bombs, which were dropped on the Japanese cities of Hiroshima and Nagasaki in August 1945, killing thousands of people outright.

Robert Oppenheimer
American 1904–1967

BOWLING REACTION!

Ask an older relative to take you ten-pin bowling. It's not just fun, it'll show you how a nuclear chain reaction can work, especially if you are lucky enough to strike ten. The ball may only hit one pin directly, but as that pin falls, it can knock down all the rest in turn.

78 In 1900, Max Planck worked out that heat is not radiated in a smooth flow, but in tiny chunks of energy that he called quanta. Albert Einstein realized that all radiation works like this – and that chunks of energy are particles. So a ray of light is streams of particles, not just waves, as everyone thought.

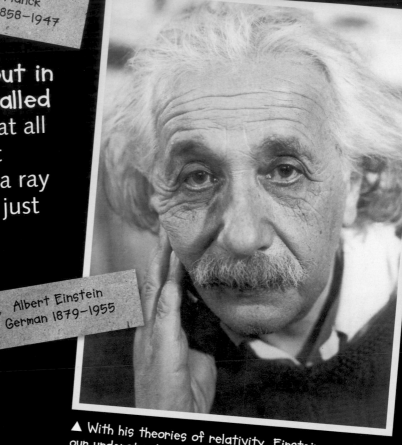

Albert Einstein
German 1879–1955

▲ With his theories of relativity, Einstein overturned our understanding of the nature of time and space.

TRUE OR FALSE?

1. A ray of light is made up of particles.
2. The speed of light can vary.
3. Gravity bends space and time.
4. Paul Dirac's theory was called quantum engines.

Answers:
1. True 2. False, the speed of light is always the same 3. True 4. False, it was called quantum mechanics

79 Speed is always measured compared to something, so the speed of an object varies depending on what you compare it to. In 1887, Einstein showed that light is special – it travels the same speed no matter how you measure it. Speed is the distance something moves through space in a certain time. If light's speed is fixed, Einstein realized that time and space must vary instead. So time and space are not fixed – they are relative and can be distorted. This is Einstein's theory of special relativity.

80 Einstein's theory of special relativity has weird effects for things travelling near the speed of light. For example, time on board a spacecraft travelling near the speed of light would seem to run slower, and the spacecraft would appear to shrink in length and get heavier.

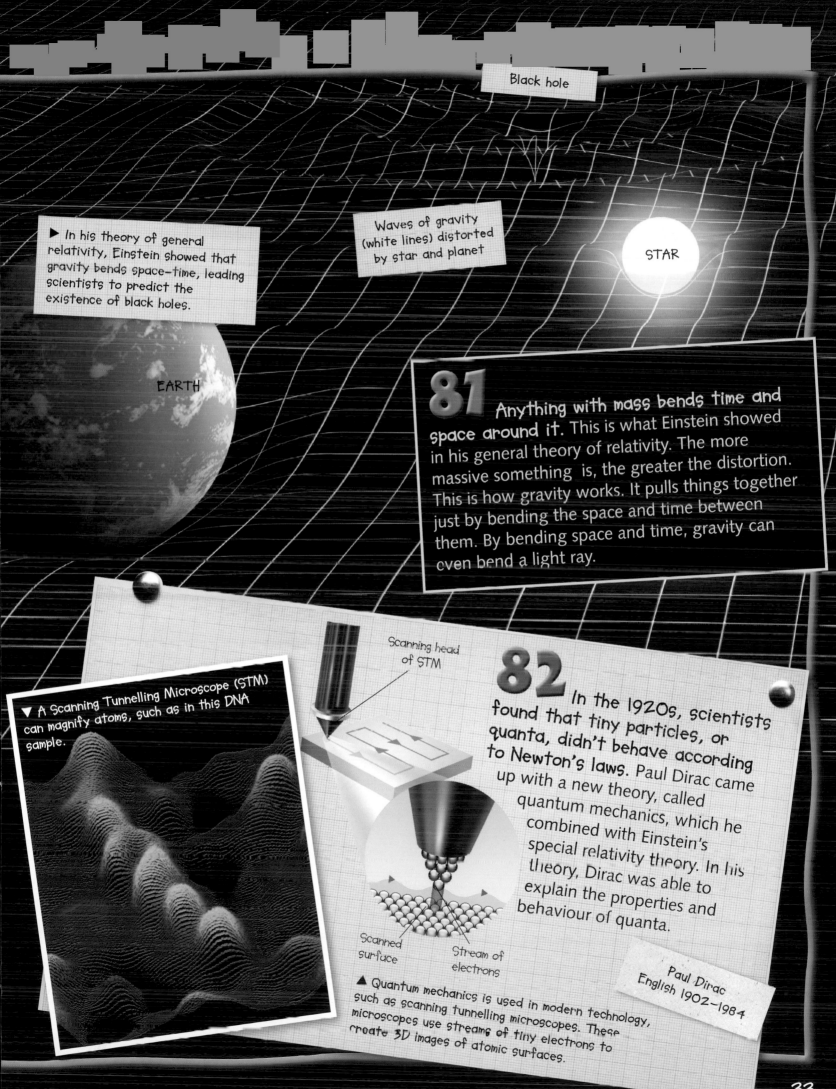

Black hole

STAR

► In his theory of general relativity, Einstein showed that gravity bends space—time, leading scientists to predict the existence of black holes.

Waves of gravity (white lines) distorted by star and planet

EARTH

81 **Anything with mass bends time and space around it.** This is what Einstein showed in his general theory of relativity. The more massive something is, the greater the distortion. This is how gravity works. It pulls things together just by bending the space and time between them. By bending space and time, gravity can even bend a light ray.

Scanning head of STM

▼ A Scanning Tunnelling Microscope (STM) can magnify atoms, such as in this DNA sample.

82 **In the 1920s, scientists found that tiny particles, or quanta, didn't behave according to Newton's laws.** Paul Dirac came up with a new theory, called quantum mechanics, which he combined with Einstein's special relativity theory. In his theory, Dirac was able to explain the properties and behaviour of quanta.

Scanned surface

Stream of electrons

Paul Dirac
English 1902—1984

▲ Quantum mechanics is used in modern technology, such as scanning tunnelling microscopes. These microscopes use streams of tiny electrons to create 3D images of atomic surfaces.

star gazers

83 A century ago, astronomers began to wonder if faint clouds in space called nebulae were actually distant galaxies. But were the stars within them really dim or just far away? To find out, astronomers looked for stars of varying brightness called cepheids. Slow varying cepheids are bright, so if they look dim, they must be far away.

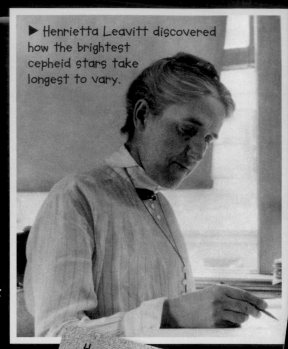

► Henrietta Leavitt discovered how the brightest cepheid stars take longest to vary.

Henrietta Swan Leavitt
American 1868–1921

◄ Andromeda was the first galaxy identified using cepheids.

84 In 1923, Edwin Hubble spotted a cepheid in the Andromeda nebula. It took a month to vary in brightness, so by Leavitt's scale it had to be 7000 times brighter than the Sun – and a million trillion kilometres away. So Andromeda must be a separate galaxy. Astronomers know now it is just one of 500 billion or so!

Edwin Hubble
American 1889–1953

▲ Edwin Hubble making observations at the Mount Wilson telescope in California, USA.

85 In 1931, Hubble found that the further away galaxies are, the redder they are. They are redder or 'red-shifted' because light waves are stretched out behind an object that is zooming away from us, just like sound drops in pitch after a car speeds past. So, the further a galaxy is from Earth, the faster it is moving away from us.

Georges Lemaître
Belgian 1894–1966

Arno Penzias
German–American
Born 1933

86

If galaxies are speeding apart now, they must have been closer together in the past. So the Universe is expanding. In the 1920s, Alexander Friedmann and Georges Lemaître suggested that the Universe was once just a tiny point that swelled like a giant explosion. One critic called the idea the Big Bang, and the name stuck.

87

Although the Big Bang theory caught on, there wasn't much proof. Then Arno Penzias and Robert Wilson picked up a faint buzz of radio signals from all over the sky. Astronomers believe that this buzz, called the Cosmic Microwave Background, is the faint afterglow of the Big Bang.

Robert Woodrow Wilson
American Born 1936

Alexander Friedmann
Russian 1888–1925

QUIZ

1. What was the first galaxy to be discovered beyond the Milky Way?
2. What is the theory of the origin of the Universe called?
3. What were pulsars jokingly called?

Answers:
1. The Andromeda Galaxy
2. The Big Bang
3. Little green men

▲ When Burnell first detected the radio pulses from pulsars, the stars were jokingly called 'little green men'.

Dame Jocelyn Bell Burnell
Northern Irish Born 1943

88

In 1967, Jocelyn Bell Burnell picked up strange radio pulses from certain stars. These pulsing stars, or pulsars, are actually tiny stars spinning at incredible speeds. They were once giant stars that have since collapsed to make a super-dense star just a few kilometres across.

Plan for life

89 **Gregor Mendel wanted to know why some living things look like their parents and why others look different.** In the 1860s, he experimented with pea flowers and their pollen to see which ones gave green peas and which ones gave yellow. Characteristics such as colour, he suggested, are passed to offspring by factors – which we now call genes.

Gregor Mendel
Austrian 1822–1884

▼ Chromosomes are the X-shaped bundles of DNA coiled up in the nucleus of a living cell.

Cell

Thomas Hunt Morgan
American 1866–1945

90 **In the 1900s, Thomas Hunt Morgan experimented with fruit flies.** He showed that genes are linked to tiny bundles in living cells called chromosomes. By removing materials from a bacterial cell one by one, Oswald Avery later found the one material it needed to pass on characteristics – DNA.

Oswald Avery
Canadian-American
1877–1955

Cell nucleus contains chromosomes

Rosalind Franklin
English 1920–1958

91 **Scientists thought DNA's ability to pass on characteristics lay in its shape.** Inspired by X-rays taken by Rosalind Franklin, Francis Crick and James Watson worked out in 1953 that the DNA molecule is a double helix (spiral). It's like a twisted rope ladder with two long strands either side linked by thousands of 'rungs'.

▲ The characteristics in this family group are clear to see, and have been passed on by DNA.

James Watson
American Born 1928

Francis Crick
English 1916–2004

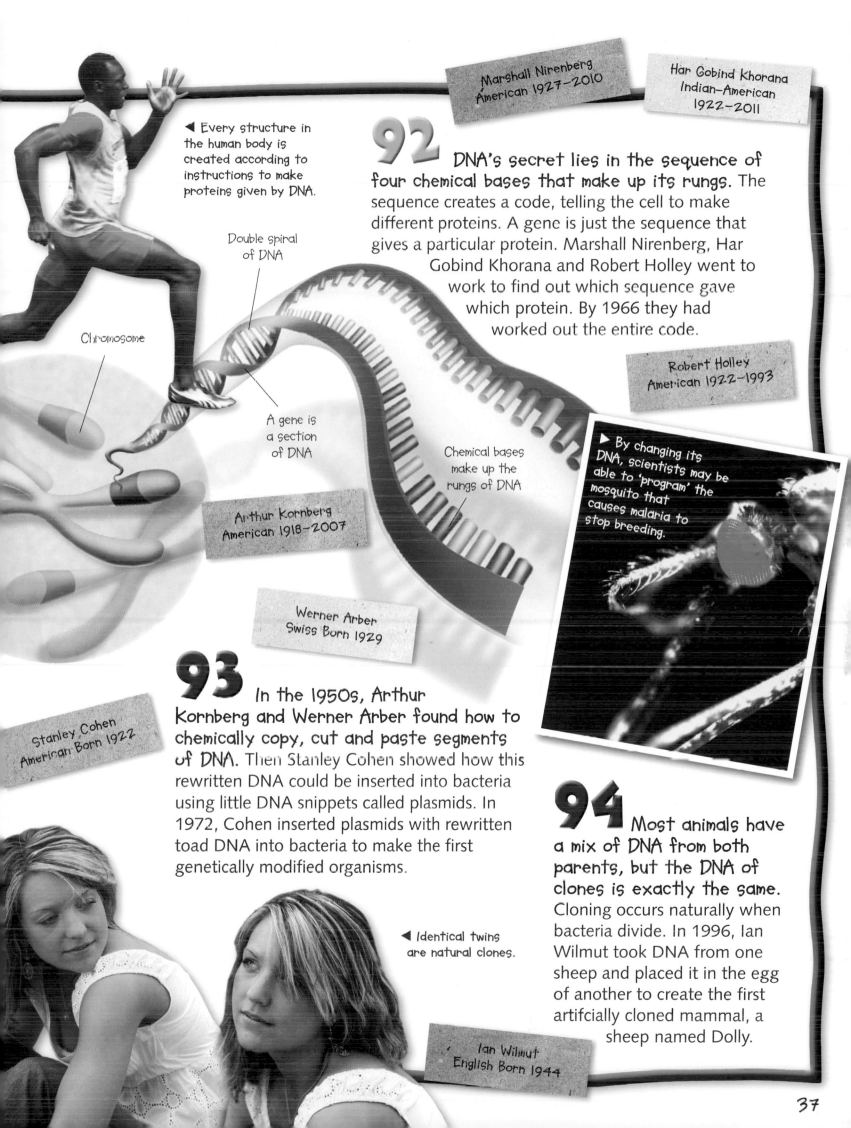

◄ Every structure in the human body is created according to instructions to make proteins given by DNA.

Double spiral of DNA

Chromosome

A gene is a section of DNA

Chemical bases make up the rungs of DNA

Marshall Nirenberg
American 1927–2010

Har Gobind Khorana
Indian–American
1922–2011

92 DNA's secret lies in the sequence of four chemical bases that make up its rungs. The sequence creates a code, telling the cell to make different proteins. A gene is just the sequence that gives a particular protein. Marshall Nirenberg, Har Gobind Khorana and Robert Holley went to work to find out which sequence gave which protein. By 1966 they had worked out the entire code.

Robert Holley
American 1922–1993

Arthur Kornberg
American 1918–2007

► By changing its DNA, scientists may be able to 'program' the mosquito that causes malaria to stop breeding.

Werner Arber
Swiss Born 1929

Stanley Cohen
American Born 1922

93 In the 1950s, Arthur Kornberg and Werner Arber found how to chemically copy, cut and paste segments of DNA. Then Stanley Cohen showed how this rewritten DNA could be inserted into bacteria using little DNA snippets called plasmids. In 1972, Cohen inserted plasmids with rewritten toad DNA into bacteria to make the first genetically modified organisms.

94 Most animals have a mix of DNA from both parents, but the DNA of clones is exactly the same. Cloning occurs naturally when bacteria divide. In 1996, Ian Wilmut took DNA from one sheep and placed it in the egg of another to create the first artifcially cloned mammal, a sheep named Dolly.

◄ Identical twins are natural clones.

Ian Wilmut
English Born 1944

Frontiers of science

96

By creating the World Wide Web in 1989, Tim Berners-Lee transformed the way the world communicates. The World Wide Web made the Internet accessible to everyone, anywhere in the world. It worked by turning computer output into web pages that could be read and displayed by any computer.

▲ Hawking suggested that the Big Bang might be a black hole in reverse, expanding from a singularity.

95

Stephen Hawking's work on black holes in space changed our understanding of the Universe. Black holes are places where gravity is so powerful that it draws in even light. At the centre is a minute point called a singularity.

97

Light is the fastest thing in the Universe. But in 2001 Lene Vestergaard Hau slowed it to a standstill by shining it through sodium atoms in a special cold state called a Bose-Einstein Condensate (BEC). In a BEC, atoms are so inactive there is nothing for particles of light to interact with, forcing them to slow down.

98

Brian Greene and Michio Kaku are working on a theory that ties together all our ideas about the Universe, matter and energy. They believe everything is made of tiny strings of energy called superstrings. Just as a violin string can make different notes, so a superstring creates particles by vibrating in different ways.

▲ In 2010, Venter created the world's first man-made living cell.

99

Craig Venter was one of many scientists involved in mapping the entire sequence of genes in human DNA. He is also sampling the oceans for micro-organisms to see just how varied DNA is.

100

Scientists explain how forces such as electromagnetic radiation are transmitted by tiny messenger particles known as bosons. But they don't know why things are heavy and have mass, and why they take force to get going and stop. Peter Higgs suggested it could be down to a mystery particle now called the Higgs boson.

▼ Scientists are trying to find the Higgs boson with a massive underground machine at CERN in Switzerland, where they smash atoms together at incredible speeds.

QUIZ

1. What would you find at the centre of a black hole?
2. What's the slowest speed light can travel?
3. Where is CERN?

Answers:
1. A singularity 2. A complete stop 3. Switzerland

Index

Page numbers in **bold** refer to main entries, those in *italics* refer to illustrations